fingerprints
of grace

fingerprints
of grace

A Tribute to the Ten Dead Men Who
Left Their Imprint on My Soul

ERIC LUDY

Ellerslie PRESS
WINDSOR, COLORADO

FINGERPRINTS OF GRACE
© 2015 by Eric Ludy

Published by Ellerslie Press
Windsor, Colorado
Ellerslie.com

Scripture taken from the King James Version®. Public Domain.

Artwork by Christy Osborne.

ISBN-10: 1943592101
ISBN-13: 9781943592104

Printed in the United States of America.

EricLudy.com

Contents

A Father's Imprint

a word before

If a man were likened to a block of clay, then the fingerprints indelibly evidenced in the pressed clay of his life would indicate who is most responsible for the shape he is currently in.

My father's fingerprints are all over me. I am my father's son and proud to be so. I could write an entire book just about my father. However, this is not that book. My purpose in this little literary work is to help enunciate not the living men who most impacted my life, but the dead ones.

But a short dedication — although it doesn't do my father justice — is necessary. For in a book that intends to pay proper tribute, how can I overlook my earthly daddy in the process of throwing out bouquets of gratitude to the men who most impacted my life? After all, it is my precious daddy's noble purpose, heavenly ethic, righteous manner, and Christ-like character that has proven the most significant thumbprint in my life's clay.

I am proud to be a Ludy, the son of Winston, the firstborn little boy of a noble man. It was his manhood that set the stage for me to recognize the grandeur of the manhood inside these upcoming pages.

Discipled By Dead Guys

In many ways I'm a man discipled by dead guys.

I've always felt like a puzzle piece that got thrown into the wrong box and now doesn't really know where he fits. Am I supposed to be alive right now? Or was I from the puzzle box labeled 1832? I've dreamed of journeying to China with Hudson Taylor, sitting in the Metropolitan Tabernacle and hearing Spurgeon preach, or even venturing into the throes of East End London next to William Booth.

But, alas, I was born in the rather spiritually dead year of 1970.

I have grown up in the age of morally failing pastors and imbecilic T.V. preachers. If you are a young man like me, born in 1970, looking for a spiritual hero, then, well, you might need to bypass the local Christian bookstore and, instead, head to your grandparent's attic and start perusing those old boxes marked "Great Great Granddad's books."

I'm not saying that a book written nowadays can't have "the stuff of old" packaged inside of it. It's just that there seems to be a damper pedal on modern Christianity.

There is a luster missing — and all the volume knobs seem broken and unable to bring the full volume to truth.

And yes, that is a self-criticism. For I write books too, and yes, I live "nowadays."

So, back to the idea of "being discipled by dead guys" ...

There were nights I'd lie awake and beg God to give me just five minutes with C.T. Studd, just so I could hear someone speak these things out loud for my natural ears to hear in this present day in order to insure that I wasn't crazy. Oh, to witness Müller's faith, to sit in Tozer's study as he prepared his weekly sermon, or to pray alongside John Hyde!

One of my great desires was to meet Richard Wurmbrand and Leonard Ravenhill before they died. I was close, but was never able to. I wanted to talk with men who suffered, men who stood strong amidst their generation, men who were uncompromising. But it would appear that God has asked me (and many of you reading this) to believe even though we haven't seen — to stand even though we have never personally met others who have stood as God is asking us to in this generation.

So, without further ado ... I would like to introduce you to the ten modern mighty men of God who have most impacted my life.

Leonard Ravenhill

traveling preacher, acclaimed author

Ravenhill's moxie has moved me. It has steeled my spine. His willingness to say and do the hard things has been to me a picture of a true man of God. His simple life, combined with his message of full consecration, is a pattern for me to this day. His book *Why Revival Tarries* ranks among the top ten books I've ever read.

Richard Wurmbrand

pastor, author, founder of
the Voice of the Martyrs

Wurmbrand's daring stand in Romania for the integrity of the Gospel of Jesus Christ is an elixir to my soul. When every other pastor sat trembling in the face of communist persecution, Wurmbrand stood up and spoke. It cost him everything. But he wiped the spit from off the face of Christ. His loving deportment while being tortured in prison is also of great significance in my discipleship. Wurmbrand has been my tutor in better understanding both the joy and perseverance possible in the face of Christian suffering.

C.T. Studd

pioneer missionary, all-around stud
(pun intended)

A man among males. I've never heard such a growl, such a grit, or such a thunderous soul for the glory of God. When I read about Studd's life and read his writings, my soul resonated with a shout. If I could pick just one man in modern Christian history who I would model my life after, it would be Studd. This man's life choices bring such conviction to my life. His entire givenness to the sustaining hand of Christ is a shot of spiritual adrenaline into my heart. And the fact that he changed the face of modern missions through his audacious risk-taking venture into the most dangerous part of Africa causes the man in me to nod in respectful, whole-hearted approval.

Charles Spurgeon

considered to be the
"Prince of Preachers"

Spurgeon's forceful eloquence of Gospel truth is moving
to my soul. His rare ability to enunciate truth with
majestic language and epic scale has been one of the
prime sources of my passion for the grandeur of Christian
expression to return to the stage of time. I can't tell you
how many times I've turned to Spurgeon in an hour of
wrestling, only to have him turn me back to my King
Jesus with a thunderous exclamation: "Do not turn to
me for life, Eric Ludy, but turn instead to the Fountain
of Life, Jesus Christ!"

18

A.W. Tozer

pastor, renowned author

While in college, it was Tozer's book *The Pursuit of God* that first drew me into the deeper waters of soul longing. A thirst for time in the Almighty's presence was awakened, and the men that Tozer listed as his mentors quickly became my own. And, once again, nearly ten years later, it was Tozer's short little book *The Divine Conquest* (ironically the sequel to *The Pursuit of God*) that proved one of the single most important books in my entire life.

Rees Howells

pioneer of persistent prayer

The man was definitely odd within his generation, but it was the good sort of oddness. His faith moved mountains and threw them into the sea. His prayers brought sweeping revival to Africa and stopped Hitler's death hammer in its tracks. His deep intimacy with God has inspired thousands — the world was certainly not worthy of this amazing man. The prayer college he founded has been the pattern for Ellerslie since its inception.

Hudson Taylor

renowned missionary to China, author

This man was a pure marvel. He was hallmarked by an indomitable strength of soul that would not budge from its position of faith, no matter the testing. He was unshakeable, immovable, and unstoppable. His stories of the China Inland Mission inspire my soul to action, and his teaching has equipped me to really live out the exchanged life of Christ.

William Booth

pastor, preacher, reformer, founder of the
Salvation Army

This man was a true chief in the Body of Christ. He led
his flock to storm hell's gates, fearlessly and with intrepid
courage. He didn't fear what man could do to him. He
reveled in the revilement and received the rotten tomatoes
to the face with a shout of praise. The heavenly blend of
compassion for the weak and conviction to defend the
truth was lived out with such majesty and grace within
his lifetime. Throughout history, perhaps none other
than William Booth demonstrated more vividly the true
power of leaping for joy when falsely accused.

George Müller

pastor, man of prayer, father of the faith, orphan advocate, author

How many times have I thought of Müller when the natural realm seemed defiant against my prayers and the moment of need was upon me? When I growl within my soul, "Watch what my God will do!" it's the Müller-inspired side of me that is talking. This man walked out the true life of faith, and that not alone. He walked it with a thousand orphans under his care. And he proved that when you open your mouth wide, God will certainly fill it. Müller demonstrated that life's necessities are nothing more than God's opportunity to shine.

John "Praying" Hyde

missionary to India,
man of Gethsemanic prayer

Hyde prayed. He prayed, and then he prayed some more. This man refused to stop praying until the answer came. His burden — the lost in India — never left him. It followed him around throughout the day and pressed him back to his knees the moment he would rise back up. He was a picture of a living sacrifice, wholly pleasing unto his God. When I think of modeling a prayer life, I gulp, and then I look to John Hyde for a pattern. The world is not the same due to this man's diligence in the prayer closet.

The Honorable Mentions

And what shall I more say? For the time would fail me to tell of

Major Ian Thomas
George Whitefield
Keith Green
David Wilkerson
Jim and Elizabeth Elliot
William Wilberforce
William Carey
Brother Yun
Gladys Aylward
D.L. Moody
John Knox
David Livingstone
David Brainerd
John G. Paton
E.M. Bounds
Eric Liddell
Paris Reidhead
John Wesley
John and Betty Stam

Oswald Chambers
R.A. Torrey
Edward Payson
Robert Murray McCheyne
Evan Roberts
Amy Carmichael
and Andrew Murray

who through faith subdued kingdoms, wrought righteousness, obtained promises, stopped the mouths of lions, quenched the violence of fire, escaped the edge of the sword, out of weakness were made strong, waxed valiant in fight, and turned to flight the armies of the aliens.

May men and women such as are listed here once against stride forth onto the stage of time. God knows we need them now!

About the Author

There were three things growing up that Eric Ludy declared he would never become: a teacher, a missionary, and a pastor. He became all three. In a vain attempt to gain some credibility he also became a writer. But seventeen books later, he's admitted that this plan backfired big time — the messages contained in his books have led to more scorn than the other three combined. Ludy is the president of Ellerslie Mission Society, the teaching pastor at the Church at Ellerslie, and the lead instructor in the Ellerslie Discipleship Training. He is descended from seven generations of pastors, totally uncool, somewhat skinny, and in Japan supposedly his last name means "Nerd." But, that said, he is clothed in the shed blood of His beloved Savior; Leslie, his wife of twenty years, still laughs at his jokes; and his six kids think he is Superman (or at least Clark Kent). So, all is well with the author of this book. He calls Windsor, Colorado home, but longs for his real home in Heaven where being a "fool for Christ" finally will be realized to be the most brilliant life-decision any human has ever made.

EricLudy.com

More Books from Eric Ludy

Romance, Relationships, & Purity
When God Writes Your Love Story
When Dreams Come True
Meet Mr. Smith
A Perfect Wedding
The First 90 Days of Marriage
Teaching True Love to a Sex-at-13 Generation
It Takes a Gentleman and a Lady

Godly Manhood
God's Gift to Women
Christian Living & Discipleship
When God Writes Your Life Story
The Bravehearted Gospel
Heroism

Prayer
Wrestling Prayer

Memoirs & Confessions
Are These Really My Pants?
Evolution of the Pterodactyl
The Bold Return of the Dunces
Fingerprints of Grace

EricLudy.com

DISCOVER MORE
FROM THE AUTHOR

SERMONS

Unashamed Gospel Thunder.

Listen now: Ellerslie.com/sermons

CONFERENCES

Come expectant. Leave transformed.

Learn more: Ellerslie.com/conferences

DISCIPLESHIP TRAINING

A set apart season to become firmly
planted in Christ.

Learn more: Ellerslie.com/training

READ MORE FROM ERIC LUDY

EricLudy.com

Made in the USA
San Bernardino, CA
07 November 2015